I0006957

SCRUM
MASTERY

Fourth Edition

*A Practical Guide to the Mastery
of Scrum Framework*

INTERNATIONAL SCRUM
ASSEMBLY™

https://www.scrumassembly.org

To our students, volunteers, and employees.

CONGRATULATIONS

C ongratulations on your decision to invest in yourself and your future!

This is the first chapter of a journey that will teach you the essentials of the *Scrum Framework*; a framework that is used to create innovative products and services. Scrum is based on a small set of core values, principles, and techniques that collectively form the Scrum Framework. Scrum is lightweight, simple to understand, and difficult to master[1]. This book is meticulously designed to provide you with a step-by-step guide to those difficulties while retaining its inherent simplicity. At the end of this journey, you will learn everything you need to master the Scrum Framework, and you will be ready to pass the official Scrum Certification Exam.

This book gives you a 50% discount on the official Scrum Certification Exam that can be redeemed at https://www.scrumassembly.org/book_discount. Upon passing the official exam, you will be granted an accredited Scrum Certificate that will open up new opportunities in your career!

ABOUT INTERNATIONAL SCRUM ASSEMBLY ™

International Scrum Assembly™ is a consortium of professional Scrum trainers and accreditors which is assembled with a vision to provide comprehensive training, examinations, and certifications to improve the profession of software delivery using the principles of Scrum and the Agile Manifesto[2]. We empower individuals around the globe to build and advance their careers while creating outstanding products and services to please their customers. Following in the footsteps of our founder and pioneer of Scrum.org, Ken Schwaber[3], our mission is to transform our profession to meet the demands of the increasingly complex world that we now live in. To do that, we must rely on increasingly sophisticated technologies, products, and genuinely agile processes to create them.

Scrum is an open Project Management Framework, and yet it has been extremely time consuming and expensive to obtain Scrum certification. A small number of profit-driven Scrum Certification Programs in the market left professionals with no option other than to make extensive time commitments and to pay expensive fees before they are allowed to take the official exam and get certified. International Scrum Assembly™ is founded to address this problem; we empower professionals coming from different backgrounds around the globe to quickly master the essentials of Scrum and get certified without having to make unreasonable time commitments or to pay unjustifiable fees. Our purpose is to bring agility to Scrum Certification process itself and return this open Project Management Framework back to whom it belongs: YOU!

We offer four distinct programs custom tailored for your specific needs: (1) International Scrum Master® Certificate or ISM®, (2) International Scrum Team Member® Certificate or ISTM®, (3) International Scrum Product Owner® Certificate or ISPO® and (4) International Scrum Executive® or ISE®.

International Scrum Assembly™ would not be where it is today without the hard work and support of its volunteers and employees and most important of all, professionals like you. On behalf of our family, we Thank You! Feel free to reach out to me if you have any questions or feedback.

Abraham White
Co-Founder & Managing Director

abraham@scrumassembly.org

Abraham

WE ARE ON A MISSION!

N olan Bushnell[4], the founder of Atari, came up with an aphorism: "All the best games are easy to learn and difficult to master."

Take Guitar Hero as an example. You can learn it today; it is as simple as matching notes that scroll on-screen to colored fret buttons on the controller. But if you want to master it, then you have to learn things like how to strum in both directions, timing of the hammer-ons, using your Star Power, and most important of all, you have to learn how to play well with your bandmates. What you need is practice, practice, and more practice; out there with your bandmates, not in a classroom!

Take football as another example. You can learn it today; it is as simple as moving the ball towards the opposition's end-zone/goal. But if you want to master it, then you have to learn things like passing, shielding, tackling, shooting, and most important of all, you have to learn how to play well with your teammates. What you need is practice, practice, and more practice; out there in the field, not in a classroom!

Scrum is no different. You can learn Scrum today; fundamentals of Scrum are so simple and common sense that anyone can learn it quickly and effectively. But if you want to master it, then you have to learn how to apply Scrum Framework in a real work environment, deliver a real project with real deadlines, and most important of all, you have to learn how to work well with your co-workers. What you need is practice, practice, and more practice; out there on the job, not in a classroom!

Then, why does Scrum require high prices in thousands of dollars and extensive time commitment for training and certification? The fact is, there is no good reason at all — other than companies making a profit out of your hopes and dreams for a better career.

International Scrum Assembly™ is founded to address this problem.

We are on a mission to open-source Scrum training & certification so that; first, you learn easily at your own pace and in the comfort of your own home; second, you prove officially that you obtained it without breaking the bank; third, you practice on the job so that you can truly master it. With this mission in mind, we developed high-quality training material that teaches you the core of Scrum, and we offer it for free. We developed practice exam questions that prepare you for the official exam, and we offer for free. Finally, we developed accredited certification programs, and we priced them as low as possible.

We believe Scrum is good for our planet; as more people can afford Scrum training and certification, more projects, more companies, and more countries will benefit from the time-proven effectiveness of Agile and Scrum framework. This way, together, we make our planet a better place.

International Scrum Assembly™

CONTENTS

CHAPTER 1: WHAT IS SCRUM?

Scrum is an Agile[5] project management framework for developing innovative products and services. It is used to address complex problems, while productively and creatively delivering products of the highest possible value. Scrum is not a technique or a definitive method; it is rather a framework within which teams can employ various processes, techniques, and methods based on the specific needs of their unique situation.

Simply put, you begin by creating a *product backlog* that is a prioritized list of the features and other capabilities. Product Backlog allows you to always work on the most important work items first. When you run out of resources (e.g., time, people), any work that didn't get picked up or completed will automatically be less important than the work that is picked up or completed. The work itself is performed in short, time-boxed *iterations*, which usually range from one to four weeks. During each iteration, a self-organizing, *cross-functional team* does all of the work (e.g., designing, building, testing). Typically, the number of work items in the product backlog is significantly larger than the team's capacity to deliver in one iteration. At the beginning of each iteration, the team *plans* and decides which high-priority subset of the product backlog will be delivered in the upcoming iteration. At the end of each iteration, the team has a potentially shippable product (or an increment of the product). If releasing after each iteration isn't appropriate, then multiple iterations can be bundled and released together[7].

△△△

APPLICATIONS OF SCRUM

Scrum has been used worldwide extensively and applied across various use cases including but not limited to: research and identify markets, technologies, and product capabilities; develop and release products and enhancements as frequently as many times per day; maintain and sustain products, systems, and other operational environments. Further, Scrum has been used to develop software (embedded and otherwise), hardware, networks of interacting functions, autonomous vehicles, schools, government, non-profit organizations, marketing, operations, and almost everything we use in our daily lives.

ΔΔΔ

FUNDAMENTAL SCRUM TRADE-OFFS

There are four fundamental trade-offs defined by the Agile Manifesto[8] that Scrum Framework implements:

1. Individuals and interactions OVER processes and tools

2. Working software OVER comprehensive documentation

3. Customer collaboration OVER contract negotiation

4. Responding to change OVER following a plan

Furthermore, there are three main focus areas that the Scrum Framework implements:

1. <u>Focus on value:</u> Everything that is done with the *Agile Mindset* focuses on the value it creates. If there is value, then do it. If there is no value, then don't do it.

2. <u>Focus on collaboration:</u> Scrum Framework focuses on teaming the people with the right skills and the right mindset for

creative collaboration by providing the right cultural environment to enable and amplify strong collaboration.

3. Focus on adaptability: Scrum Framework deals with the fact that requirements do change quickly and frequently. Therefore, teams re/de-prioritize existing work when it is realized that it is not valuable. For that reason, the *Agile Mindset* gives special emphasis on adaptability.

CHAPTER 2: WHO USES SCRUM AND WHY?

Any team who has a complex project uses Scrum so that the team delivers results faster by prioritizing long to-do lists into manageable work items along with improved teamwork and crystal-clear communication. In particular, Scrum has transformed the process of software development. According to recent studies, 76% of all software companies, regardless of industry, use Scrum or its variants. The main reason behind this broad adoption across multiple industries is because organizations are repeatedly delighting their customers by giving them precisely what they want in a fast and predictable manner. This allows organizations to test various options quickly, fail fast, and double-down on the option that succeeds, which eventually leads to an improved return on investment (ROI). Furthermore, organizations can reduce costs by eliminating waste and preventing dysfunction.

Figure 1: Benefits of Scrum

It is important to note that Scrum is not a silver bullet; however, Scrum can enable you and your organization to please your customers by improving teams' delivery speed, increasing confidence, reducing cost and improving ROI. Scrum framework is simple; however, it would be a misconception to assume that Scrum is easy to apply. Scrum doesn't prescribe answers for your process questions; instead, it empowers and enables teams to ask and answer their own questions, the right questions. Scrum doesn't provide you with a definitive solution to all of your organizational challenges; instead, it makes the dysfunction and wastes visible so that, as leaders of your organizations, you can take the initiative to fix them. For that reason, Scrum enables organizations to realize and exceed their true potential.

CHAPTER 3: SCRUM FRAMEWORK VS WATERFALL METHOD?

W aterfall Method, also known as Gantt Method, was invented by Henry Gantt around 1910 originally for manufacturing and construction industries. In this method, every single step in a project is planned and written down in detail (e.g., every milestone, delivery date, tasks, features, etc.). Further, the Waterfall Method followed a sequential, linear process and was the most popular version of the system development lifecycle (SDLC) until the 1990s. There are five stages in the Waterfall Method and development teams cannot move onto the next stage without completing the previous stage. Also, development teams cannot go back to a prior stage without starting the whole process from the beginning. Waterfall Method worked very well for the simple, unchanging project.

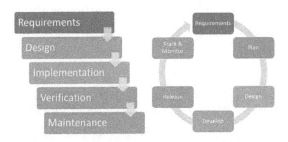

Figure 2: Waterfall Model vs. Scrum Framework

Waterfall Method's linear and rigid nature was best suited for the manufacturing and construction industries for which it was originally designed as they are highly structured and requirements don't change and can be too expensive to incorporate. However, the same linear and rigid nature of the Waterfall Model introduced challenges in the software industry where requirements change very quickly and frequently; working software needs to be delivered rapidly and frequently in the SDLC to get customer feedback; there may be a high amount of uncertainty; problems are complex, and solutions are object-oriented.

CHAPTER 4: SCRUM VALUES AND PRINCIPLES

S crum is a simple framework for organizing, managing and delivering work. Using this framework, your organization creates its unique implementation of relevant engineering practices to solve your own complex problems.

SCRUM VALUES

Application of Scrum can only be possible if all participants share the same set of core *values:* honesty, integrity, transparency, respect, courage, focus, commitment, trust, and collaboration. Many organizations do not pay attention to these values; however, it is essential to establish an organizational culture that embodies these Scrum *values* for the practical application and execution of the Scrum framework.

ΔΔΔ

SCRUM PRINCIPLES –THE NORTH STAR

There are 12 *principles* from the Agile Manifesto[10] that constitute the foundation of the Scrum Framework. These principles should strictly be followed while applying Scrum Framework to your projects. Furthermore, these principles are the North Star of any agile team. They will guide you and your organization at any decision point.

1. Our highest priority is to satisfy the customer through early and continuous delivery of valuable software.

2. Welcome changing requirements, even late in development. Agile processes harness change for the customer's competitive advantage.

3. Deliver working software frequently, from a couple of weeks to a couple of months, with a preference to the shorter timescale.

4. Business people and developers must work together daily throughout the project.

5. Build projects around motivated individuals. Give them the environment and support they need, and trust them to get the job done.

6. The most efficient and effective method of conveying information to and within a de-

velopment team is a face-to-face conversation.

7. Working software is the primary measure of progress.

8. Agile processes promote sustainable development. The sponsors, developers, and users should be able to maintain a constant pace indefinitely.

9. Continuous attention to technical excellence and good design enhances agility.

10. Simplicity--the art of maximizing the amount of work not done--is essential.

11. The best architectures, requirements, and designs emerge from self-organizing teams.

12. At regular intervals, the team reflects on how to become more effective, then tunes and adjusts its behavior accordingly.

These principles are the core guidelines that are actively used to apply the Scrum framework. They are non-negotiable and should be internalized and organically applied by Scrum Masters, Scrum Product Owners, Scrum Team Members as well as Scrum Executives.

CHAPTER 5: SCRUM ROLES

S crum consists of one or more *Scrum Teams* each of which has four specific Scrum *roles*:

1. Development Team Member
2. Scrum Master
3. Product Owner
4. Scrum Executive.

Each of these roles has a well-defined set of responsibilities and closely interact with each other to deliver results successfully.

∆∆∆

SCRUM TEAM MEMBER

Scrum Development Team is a cross-functional team that consists of individuals coming from different backgrounds such as architect, designer, programmer, tester, research scientist, data scientist, database engineer, database administrator, program manager, and so on. Every member of this diverse cross-functional team is called Scrum Team Member. The team is typically 9 (+/-2) people in size, and the team should collectively have all the skills required to deliver a working shippable product. International Scrum Assembly™ provides specific training and certification for Scrum Team Member: International Scrum Team Member® Certificate or ISTM®.

△△△

SCRUM MASTER

The Scrum Master is the ambassador of the Scrum *values*, *principles*, and *practices*. She/he acts as a coach and educates all team members so that they embrace Scrum *values*, *principles*, and *practices*. As a result, the team organically develops its own unique Scrum approach suited for its unique needs. The Scrum Master is also responsible for protecting the team from outside interferences by preventing unessential requests to reach the team members. It is important to note that the Scrum Master does not have any authority to exert control over the team members, and this way, it differs from the traditional project manager and functional and people manager. International Scrum Assembly™ provides specific training and certification for Scrum Masters: International Scrum Master® Certificate or ISM®.

ΔΔΔ

PRODUCT OWNER

The Product Owner is responsible for the product that will be developed. She/he is a single authority determining which features the team should build as well as their associated priority and order. Besides, the Product Owner is responsible for communicating with all stakeholders a clear vision of what the team is trying to achieve. Furthermore, the Product Owner is responsible and accountable for the overall success of the final product. International Scrum Assembly™ provides specific training and certification for Product Owners: International Scrum Product Owner® Certificate or ISPO®.

ΔΔΔ

SCRUM EXECUTIVE

The Scrum Executive is an individual who owns a particular business entity and is responsible for generating revenue and profit from the successful operations of the company. The successful operation includes, but is not limited to, creating new revenue streams by launching new lines of products or by making enhancements to existing products, improving operational efficiency to reduce operational expenses, make decisions on capital expenditures, and so on. Scrum Executive has executive decision-making powers. International Scrum Assembly™ provides specific training and certification for Scrum Executive: International Scrum Executive® or ISE®.

CHAPTER 6: SCRUM TEAMS

Scrum Team is a group of people working together to deliver the committed product. To work effectively together, it is vital that everyone in the Scrum Team follows a common goal, adheres to the same principles, and trusts and respects each other. It is also important to keep in mind that the Scrum Teams will get more and more efficient over time. Tuckman Model[11] describes the phases that high-performance Scrum Teams go through before they can function at their highest possible performance.

CHARACTERISTICS

Successful Scrum Teams have the following *characteristics*:

1. Scrum Team is accountable for the delivery
2. Scrum Team is empowered to make decisions independently
3. Scrum Team is self-organizing and self-correcting
4. Talent within the Scrum Team is diverse

and well-balanced
5. Scrum Team is atomic; it is small and self-sufficient
6. Team members work full time in the team
7. Team members follow the same goals and principles.

△△△

RULES AND NORMS

Successful Scrum Teams have the following *rules*, *norms* and *Standard Operating Procedures* (SOP) that are typically formed during the *Norming Phase* of the Tuckman Model:

1. Time, location, and duration of the *Daily Scrum Meeting*
2. Coding practices and guidelines
3. Testing practices and guidelines
4. Release practices and guidelines
5. Definition of Done (DoD) which is used to decide whether the work is finished or not
6. Internal and external tools to use.

△△△

ACCOUNTABILITY

The Scrum Team is accountable for delivering the committed product (or a shippable iteration of the product) on the committed delivery date, at high quality. Neither success nor failure is attributed to any single individual team member; the team altogether is responsible. The Scrum Team is accountable for identifying and compensating for the low-performing members. No single member of the team can be held accountable for the failure to deliver results.

△△△

SIZE OF THE SCRUM TEAM

Scrum Teams are small and self-contained, ideally having 9 (+/-2) members. Larger teams lead to *communication overhead* which reduces the effectiveness and productivity of the team. If the project is too large and complex for one Scrum Team, then the project must be split across multiple Scrum Teams with clear deliverables and ownership. The Product Owner oversees splitting the project down to smaller pieces to be owned by multiple Scrum Teams and coordinate the communication across them. For example; Jeff Bezos[13], founder and the CEO of Amazon.com, Inc., has introduced a concept of *two-pizza teams*[14] [15]. He suggested that every internal team should be small enough that it can be fed with two pizzas. Bezos understood the importance of the size of the teams: a smaller team spends less time managing timetables and keeping people up to date, and more time doing what needs to be done.

△△△

COLLOCATION

Traditional Scrum suggests that the Scrum teams must be collocated to minimize unnecessary communication overhead. This legacy concept of collocation was introduced in the late 2000s when the communication tools were not as advanced as they are today, and where the leaders of the Scrum Teams could, in fact, form a local team with reasonable effort. The world has changed since then. The reality of today is that having all employees in a single/same location is almost impossible to build or maintain. Furthermore, internet and communication technologies have advanced so much so that remote teams can work and communicate effectively even if they are not collocated.

As businesses became increasingly international in response to globalization, successful organizations are faced with the challenge of applying Scrum Framework at a global scale through Scrum teams that cannot be (and should not be) collocated. Therefore, the legacy concept of collation must be revisited in light of today's realities and capabilities.

The feedback we received from our employers is aligned with this fact: the international business environment made it necessary to build and grow international organizations. While mainstream Scrum schools continue to advise students to collocate their Scrum teams, we take a different approach here at International Scrum Assembly™. In Chapter 10, we explain in detail how you can apply the Scrum Framework effectively to international (or remote) teams. We will teach you how to internationalize your Scrum skills.

CHAPTER 7: SCRUM ACTIVITIES

Scrum Framework is implemented through a well-defined set of events and activities. Eight specific Scrum activities will be examined in this chapter.

1. Product backlog and grooming
2. Sprint planning
3. Commitment
4. Sprint execution
5. Sprint review
6. Sprint retrospective
7. Daily Scrum
8. Repeating cycle

PRODUCT BACKLOG AND GROOMING

After collecting input and insights from customers and stakeholders, the Product Owner creates the product vision. Vision is usually broad, and therefore full development cannot fit into a single iteration. *Grooming* is an activity for breaking this vision down into a small set of features and functionalities. At the end of *grooming* exercise, you have a prioritized list of features that is called the *product backlog*. Scrum recommends doing the most valuable work first. On a new product, *product backlog* items initially are the critical features required to meet the Product Owner's vision to please the customers. For existing products, *product backlog* items are usually enhancements, new features and bug fixes, technical improvements and so on. The Product Owner collaborates with customers, internal and external stakeholders to compile the *product backlog*. The Product Owner also ensures that the *product backlog* items are prioritized correctly to ensure that the most important tasks get done first. Note that the *product backlog* is a living list – it continually changes and evolves. As the business requirements and customer expectations change, the *Product Owner* refines the product backlog by adding, deleting and revising the backlog items.

∆∆∆

SPRINT PLANNING

A *sprint* starts with a *sprint planning* meeting which determines the development work to be completed during the sprint, which is called *sprint execution*, and ends with the *review* and *retrospective*. The number of work items in the *product backlog* is almost always more than the development team can complete in one sprint. Therefore, at the beginning of each sprint, the development team determines a subset of the product backlog that it believes it can achieve during the sprint. This activity is called *sprint planning*. Scrum Framework allows work to be performed in iterations each of which creates something of tangible value to the end customer. All sprints are time-boxed meaning that they always have a fixed start and end date. A new sprint starts after a completed sprint, and this cycle continues until the final product is delivered to the customer. An important rule to note is that no goal-altering changes should be permitted during a sprint. During *Sprint Planning*, the Scrum Team and the Product Owner agree on a *sprint goal* which sets the course for the sprint that is being planned.

ΔΔΔ

COMMITMENT

Scrum Team generates a *commitment* (also referred as *forecast* or *estimate*) of what they can deliver each sprint. The *commitment* helps establish mutual trust between the Product Owner and The Scrum Team as well as the Scrum Executive. Further, *commitment* supports reasonable and realistic short-term planning and decision making within the team. As part of the *commitment*, the Scrum Team creates a backlog of items during sprint planning that is called *sprint backlog*. The *sprint backlog* defines how the team plans to design, implement, test, and deliver the selected subset of tasks from the *product backlog.*

ΔΔΔ

SPRINT EXECUTION

Once the Scrum Team finishes the sprint planning and agrees on the commitment, they start to perform all of the tasks needed to get the features done – based on *Definition of Done* or (DoD). Scrum Team has full control over what order or how to do the tasks that are in the *sprint backlog*. The Scrum Team self-organizes, in whatever manner they see fit, to deliver all tasks and hence achieve the *sprint goal*. Each day during *sprint execution*, Scrum Team Members manage the flow of work by using the activities called *synchronization*, *inspection,* and *adaptive planning*. These activities constitute *Daily Scrum*. At the end of the *sprint execution,* the Scrum Team delivers a shippable product that makes incremental progress towards the Product Owner's vision.

ΔΔΔ

DAILY SCRUM

At the beginning of each day of the sprint, the Scrum Team members hold a time-boxed *daily scrum* meeting. This meeting ideally takes 15 minutes or less. It is part of the inspect-and-adapt activity. The daily scrum meeting is also known as *daily stand-up* because all team members are standing throughout the meeting to promote brevity. The *Scrum Master* facilitates the *daily scrum* during which each team member takes turns answering three main questions:

1. What did I accomplish since the last daily scrum?
2. What do I plan to do by the next daily scrum?
3. What are the obstacles that can potentially prevent me from making progress?

By answering these basic questions, everyone becomes aware of everyone else and sees the big picture of what is being built and how the team is progressing towards the *sprint goal*. Daily Scrum plays a key role in helping the Scrum Team manage the fast delivery of work during every sprint. Please note that Daily Scrum is not a brainstorming and problem-solving session; rather, it is an inspection, synchronization and adaptive planning activity.

ΔΔΔ

REPEATING CYCLE

Scrum Team completes the sprint by executing an activity called *inspect-and-adapt*. First, during an activity called *sprint review*, the stakeholders and the Scrum Team inspect the product. Second, during an activity called *sprint retrospective*, Scrum Team audits the Scrum process that is being used by the team. The outcome of these two activities goes into a feedback loop through which the Scrum Team improves not only the product being built but also the process being used.

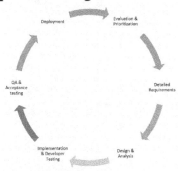

Figure 3: Iteration Details

At this point, the sprint *cycle repeats*. The Scrum Team determines the next most important set of *product backlog* items it can complete during the next *sprint*. After many sprints go through this *repeating cycle*, the *Product Owner*'s vision is realized, and the final product is created.

CHAPTER 8: USER STORIES AND REQUIREMENTS

I n Agile development, the details of the requirement are negotiated through conversations that happen continuously in a just-in-time manner so that the teams can start building the functionality and start supporting the requirements from the get-go. In the Waterfall Model, the requirements are clearly identified and locked at the beginning of the development lifecycle, but it is impossible to identify and lock all of the requirements for software development projects. The fact is when developing an innovative product, complete and clear requirements cannot possibly be created up front because the requirements by definition change as time passes and the Scrum Team learns more about the business requirements which itself is a living organism.

ΔΔΔ

PRODUCT BACKLOG ITEMS (PBIS)

For that reason, Scrum Teams do not invest significant time and resources trying to determine complete requirements up front simply because the requirements change as time passes. Instead, Scrum Teams create placeholders for the requirements that are called *Product Backlog Items* (PBIs) each of which represents a particular business value. Initially, PBIs are large and vague. Over time, through a series of conversations, PBIs are refined into a collection of small and more detailed tasks that can eventually be added to *product backlog* and picked for execution during *sprint planning*.

ΔΔΔ

USER STORIES

User Stories are simple templates that describe the expected business outcome of the *product backlog* items. What is unique about *user stories* is that they are created in a specific way so that it is consumable by both business people (e.g., Scrum Executive) and technical people (e.g., Scrum Team Member). Simply put, a *user story* tells a short story about a user using the product. It contains a name, a brief narrative as well as acceptance criteria. User stories focus on precisely what the customer wants without explaining the technical details of how to achieve it.

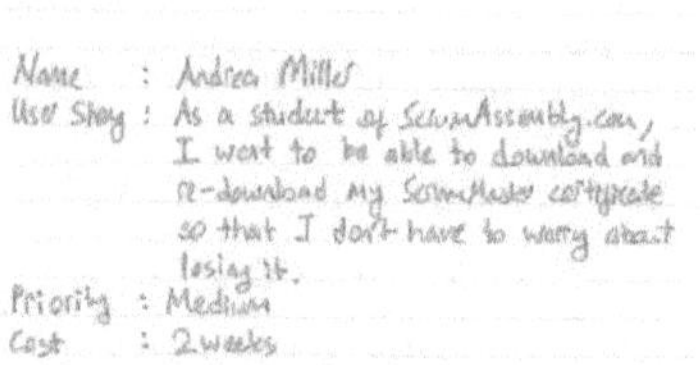

Figure 4: User story card

∆∆∆

CARDS

The *card* is very simple. People write their stories on a 3x5 inch index cards or sticky notes. It contains the user role, name, what that user is trying to achieve, and why the user is trying to achieve that goal (a.k.a. the benefit), as well as a "so that" section that explains the underlying intent. The *card* does not intend to capture all of the details that constitute the requirement. Instead, they are brief, holding a few sentences that capture the gist of the requirement. It is a placeholder for a more detailed discussion that will take place among the stakeholders under the supervision of the Product Owner and Scrum Team.

ΔΔΔ

INVEST

Bill Wake offered six criteria to create good stories[19]. INVEST is an acronym that represents these criteria: Independent, Negotiable, Valuable, Estimatable, Small and Testable. User stories should be *independent* meaning that they should be decoupled or loosely coupled with other user stories. The details of the stories should be *negotiable*. They are not a written contract. Instead, they are placeholders for more in-depth discussions. Stories must be *valuable* for a customer in a way that they should be willing to and ready to pay for it. Stories should be *estimable* by the team that is going to create them. Stories should be *small* enough to fit in *sprint planning*. Stories should be *testable* in a binary way meaning that they should either pass or fail the test.

CHAPTER 9: ADDITIONAL AGILE CONCEPTS

S crum Framework allows your team to employ various techniques that suit your particular needs and requirements. In this chapter, we discuss a few of those important Agile concepts that you may find useful.

LAST RESPONSIBLE MOMENT (LRM)

People who adopt an Agile Mindset and exercise Scrum Framework would never make a decision until the very last responsible moment. Because Scrum Framework recommends keeping your options open until the LRM, when the cost of not making a decision becomes higher than the cost of making a decision.

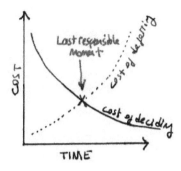

Figure 5: Last Responsible Moment (LRM)

△△△

PREDICTIVE UP-FRONT VS. ADAPTIVE JUST-IN-TIME WORK

Scrum Framework encourages up-front work. Does that mean that the planning and requirement work should be done up-front? No! Scrum is all about finding moderation and balance that is the balance between predictive up-front vs. adaptive just-in-time. The balance point should be determined in a way that maximizes the amount of ongoing adaptation and minimizes the amount of up-front prediction. Experienced Scrum Masters and Product Owners know how to strike this balance as this balance is situational and very specific to the circumstances.

△△△

WORK IN PROGRESS (WIP)

Work in Progress (WIP) refers to the work that is started but not yet finished. WIP must be adequately identified, recognized and continuously managed using the following three principles:

1. Focus on idle work, not idle workers
2. Use economically sensible batch sizes
3. Consider the cost of delay. The benefit includes but not limited to; reduced cycle time, reduced overhead, increased motivation, accelerated feedback and reduced variability.

△△△

EXPLORATION VS. EXPLOITATION

Exploration refers to times when teams choose to gain knowledge by creating prototypes, creating proof of concepts (POC) or conducting an experiment. Exploitation refers to times when teams decide to seize a particular opportunity (identified by the *exploration* stage) by creating value for customers generating revenue for the company. Teams should spend a balanced amount of time exploring and exploiting any given point in time. Typically, it is the Scrum Executive's responsibility to strike a balance between investing in exploration vs. exploitation so that resources are allocated accordingly. However, successful Scrum Product Owners do provide their recommendation to the leadership team. In some cases, Scrum Executives delegate this decision solely to Scrum Product Owners.

CHAPTER 10: COLLOCATED VS INTERNATIONAL TEAMS

I n The State of Agile Survey conducted by Col-labNet VersionOne in 2010, more than 50% of the survey respondents said they are currently using Agile with both collocated and distributed teams. In 2015, the same survey revealed that more than 82% of the respondents had distributed teams practicing Agile within their organizations[20].

Traditional Scrum suggests that the Scrum teams must be collocated to minimize unnecessary communication overhead. The world has changed since this legacy concept of collocation was intro-duced in the late 2000s. The reality of today is that having all employees in a single/same location is almost impossible to build or maintain. Further-more, the internet and communication technolo-gies have advanced so much that the teams can work and communicate effectively even if they are not collocated.

As businesses become increasingly international

in response to globalization, successful organizations are faced with the challenge of applying Scrum Framework at a global scale through Scrum teams that cannot be (and should not be) collocated. Therefore, the legacy concept of collation must be revisited in light of today's realities and capabilities. The feedback we received from our employers is aligned with this fact.

While mainstream Scrum schools continue to advice students to collocate their Scrum teams, we take a different approach here at International Scrum Assembly™. In this chapter, we explain in detail how you can apply the Scrum Framework effectively to remote teams. We will teach you how to internationalize your Scrum skills.

ΔΔΔ

COLLOCATED TEAMS

The primary reason for co-location is to maximize the team's ability to communicate in person. Alistair Cockburn[21] (age 65 years), an American computer scientist known as one of the initiators of the agile movement, coined a new term, *Osmotic Communication* defined as "Osmotic communication means that information flows into the background hearing of members of the team, so that they pick up relevant information as though by osmosis. This is normally accomplished by seating them in the same room. Then, when one person asks a question, others in the room can either tune in or tune out, contributing to the discussion or continuing with their work." Following the footsteps of Alistair Cockburn, the traditional Scrum schools of the 2000s introduced this legacy concept of collocation to realize the following benefits:

- Trust can be earned quickly
- Problems can be fixed quickly
- Clarification questions can be asked and answered quickly
- No 'us versus them' mindset
- Transfer of knowledge can be achieved quickly

ΔΔΔ

INTERNATIONAL SCRUM TEAMS

Traditional Scrum processes and strategies start to fall apart as the team distribution spans across multiple locations and across multiple time zones – which is why traditional scrum methodologies continue to advice collocated teams. However, you can, in fact, apply the Scrum framework to distributed teams by making small adjustments to your processes.

ΔΔΔ

WHAT'S A DISTRIBUTED TEAM?

There are three different types of distributed teams.

1. <u>Multi-site teams</u> have two or more collocated teams at separate locations, e.g., a company that has multiple headquarters or multiple sites that are located in different countries.

2. <u>Satellite workers</u> occur when you have most of the team co-located, but a few members are working remotely, either from home or from a different office. This is a very common team structure, especially in the software development sector.

3. <u>Remote-first</u> teams are the teams where everyone works in a separate location, usually from home. Most of the open-source projects apply this model as well as the early stage start-ups.

ΔΔΔ

ONLINE TOOLS FOR SCRUM FRAMEWORK

Scrum Teams take advantage of physical tools such as white-boards, sticky notes, chalkboards, and so on. Today, online tools are capable of replacing them in a virtual environment. International Scrum Teams utilize tools such as Quip, Slack, Asana, Microsoft Office 365, Google Apps, Zoho, OX, and many others. Some of the online tools, such as Visual Studio, have project templates specifically for Scrum Framework helping teams to organize their user stories, product backlogs, sprint execution, burn-down charts and so on.

ΔΔΔ

SCRUM OF SCRUMS

Scrum of scrums is a virtual team that consists of representatives from multiple Scrum teams. While individual Scrum teams focus on their specific deliverables; Scrum of scrum focuses on the integration of the pieces that individual Scrum teams build. It is typically used as a scaling mechanism for products that cannot be developed by a single Scrum team. The same mechanism can be utilized to coordinate across Scrum teams that are not collocated. For example; say your organization has one Scrum team in San Francisco, Palo Alto, Hyderabad,

Dublin, and New York, where they apply the Scrum Framework locally. You form a scrum of scrums virtual-team by including one representative from each team. The virtual team has regular sync up meetings to coordinate. This way, your organization can go beyond the geographical limitations of the collocated teams.

ΔΔΔ

PAIR PROGRAMMING

Pair programming is a technique that is widely used within the Scrum Framework. Traditional pair programming is about two team members sitting side-by-side and working on the same code. At first, this could be perceived as a challenge for distributed teams. However, the in-person experience can be replicated using screen-sharing features of the latest communication technologies mentioned in the previous section.

ΔΔΔ

ACCESSING A BROAD TALENT POOL

Today, business growth in the global tech sector outpaces the number of graduates of technical majors from universities worldwide. Therefore, it is difficult to find and retain high-quality technical employees. This is even more difficult if a company resists adoption of a distributed team structure. For that reason, many successful tech companies form distributed teams to get access to the talent pool at multiple locations.

ΔΔΔ

OPTIMIZING THE TEAM MIX

It is not optimal to homogenously locate separate roles in separate locations. For example; locating all of your developers in Hyderabad and all of your product managers in San Francisco is not optimal. This type of a sub-optimal setup leads to communication breakdowns and deteriorates the culture and the integrity of the teams. Every site should be organized such that it has access to a majority of the technical roles it needs to achieve its goals.

CHAPTER 11: SCRUM MASTER

The Scrum Master is one of the roles that every Scrum Team has. The Scrum Master is responsible for ensuring the correct Scrum process throughout the project. The primary focus of Scrum Masters is to help everyone in the Scrum Team to understand, adopt and apply Scrum Framework that is the *values*, *principles,* and *practices.* The Scrum Master is a coach and an advisor; helping Scrum Team Members as well as the Product Owner to operate within the Scrum Framework. The Scrum Master is a leader; helping Scrum Teams to develop their own unique Scrum approach. In this chapter, you are going to learn the unique role and responsibilities of successful Scrum Masters and how they operate in detail.

RESPONSIBILITIES OF THE SCRUM MASTER

The Scrum Master has six main responsibilities: coaching others, blocking external interferences, removing internal blockers, serving as a leader, managing the process and managing the change.

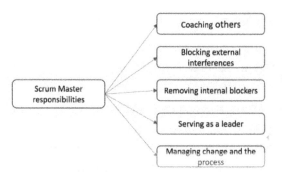

Figure 6: Scrum Master responsibilities

Let's look at each of these responsibilities in detail and understand what they mean as well as how you will apply them in your daily job as a Scrum Master.

△△△

COACHING OTHERS

In sports, a coach is a person involved in the direction, instruction and training of the operations of a sports team or individual sportspeople[25]. Similarly, The Scrum Master is a professional involved in the direction, instruction and training of the operations of The Scrum Team as a whole. He/she closely monitors the way the Scrum Framework is being used in the team and makes regular adjustments to improve the performance of the team on a continuous basis. Under the leadership of the Scrum Master, the team continually improves its performance sprint after sprint.

ΔΔΔ

BLOCKING EXTERNAL INTERFERENCES

Scrum Teams, all around the globe, are faced with plenty of external interference, constant randomization, distractions, and churn. Interference can originate from various sources including but not limited to people managers, Scrum Product Owner, Scrum Executive, partner teams, dependency teams and services, even customer representatives. No matter the source of the interference; one of the primary responsibilities of the Scrum Master is to block these distractions so that the team is shielded against randomization and therefore Scrum Team Members can focus on delivering business value in every sprint.

ΔΔΔ

REMOVING INTERNAL BLOCKERS

Scrum Teams often face blockers that negatively impact the teams' productivity. The Scrum Master takes responsibility for removing such internal blockers <u>only when</u> team members themselves are not able to remove on their own. Scrum Master has the attitude of *helping the team to solve its own problems* rather than *solving the problems for the team*. After all, successful Scrum Teams are able to solve their own problems quickly and effectively. If the team is unable to resolve the problem on its own, then Scrum Master takes the initiative and owns the problem through successful resolution.

For example, in 2015, I was the Scrum Master of a project where the team was developing a web service that calculates expected profitability and margins of a broad selection of products. The team was dependent on the availability of certain data points (e.g., demand forecast, product cost, expected discounts, etc.) at scale to serve its callers within SLA. The Scrum Team was missing its sprint goals three sprints in a row, and the team members were not able to resolve it on their own. After the third *sprint review meeting*, I realized that the team on which we were dependent had been violating their SLA causing in my Scrum Team to violate its SLA. My Scrum

Team Members had reached out to the other team but couldn't get a quick resolution. I took ownership of this conflict and worked with the Scrum Master and Product Owner of the dependent team as well as our common Scrum Executive to get this work prioritized and dependency conflict removed. When we entered the fifth sprint, the issue was resolved, and our team was back within its SLA.

ΔΔΔ

SERVING AS A LEADER

Servant leadership is a leadership philosophy in which the primary goal of the leader is to serve. This is different from traditional leadership where the leader's main focus is the thriving of their company or organization[26]. A Servant Leader shares power, and puts the needs of the employees first and helps people develop and perform as highly as possible[27]. The Scrum Master is the *servant leader* of the Scrum Team. The attitude of the Scrum Master is *what can I do to help you today* rather than *what are you going to do for me today.*

ΔΔΔ

MANAGING CHANGE AND THE PROCESS

The Scrum Master is the team's process author-ity, ensuring that the team adopts and applies the Scrum Framework throughout the project. The Scrum Master continuously improves the process after each sprint by articulating and applying the lessons learned from the previous sprint to the next sprint. Note that the Scrum Master's authority is limited to the process and not expand to hiring or firing power. Furthermore, the Scrum Master does not have the authority to dictate what tasks the Scrum Team will execute nor how the tasks are to be executed.

"To improve is to change", said Winston Church-ill, "to be perfect is to change often". The Scrum Master helps team members understand the value of *to change* and *to change often* by explaining the broad benefits of changing as well as the dangers of getting stuck in the status quo. The Scrum Frame-work can be very disruptive and uncomfortable for those teams and individuals who got stuck in the status quo. Bankwest, an Australian full-ser-vice bank based in Perth, put twenty of its senior leaders in an old bank vault in November 2018 to get them onboard with agile and stop blocking its progress[28]. A successful Scrum Master not only is in charge of managing the change but also earning people's hearts and minds to establish a strong commitment to change.

ΔΔΔ

COMPETENCIES OF THE SCRUM MASTER

Successful Scrum Masters in the market have certain common characteristics and competencies. First of all, Scrum Masters are knowledgeable and collaborative. They are curious in nature and leverage this curiosity to learn on a constant basis. They quickly earn the trust of the scrum team members as well as product owner and stakeholders by being open & transparent. They can also be very protective when needed and shield the scrum teams from distractions.

Figure 7: Competencies of Successful Scrum Masters

SCRUM MASTERS ARE KNOWLEDGEABLE

Scrum Masters have breadth as well as depth when it comes to knowledgebase; they have a *broad* understanding of the market that the business is operating at while having an in-depth knowledge of the Scrum Framework as well as the technical details of the product being built. The Scrum Master understands the technologies used by the Scrum Team, details of the product that is being built. Furthermore, even though it's not their primary responsibility, successful Scrum Masters also know how this product fits into the business model that the company is operating under as well as the positioning of this product in the market.

ΔΔΔ

SCRUM MASTERS ARE CURIOUS

Scrum Masters are curious people in nature. They ask *great questions* helping Scrum Team Members as well as other stakeholders to help them realize that they have the insight and ability to find their own answers. Many great Scrum Masters use a technique called *Socratic questioning*[29]. Socratic questioning was named after Socrates, who was a philosopher in c. 470 BCE–c. 399 BCE. Socrates believed that the disciplined practice of thoughtful questioning enables the scholar/student to examine ideas and be able to determine the validity of those ideas. Socratic questioning is a form of disciplined questioning that can be used to pursue thought in many directions and for many purposes, including: to explore complex ideas, to get to the truth of things, to open up issues and problems, to uncover assumptions, to analyze concepts, to distinguish what we know from what we do not know, to follow out logical consequences of thought or to control discussions[30].

Successful Scrum Masters use another similar technique called *precision questioning* to get to the root of any particular group discussion. Precision questioning (PQ) is an intellectual toolkit for critical thinking[31] and problem-solving, grew out of a collaboration between Dennis Matthies and Dr. Monica Worline, while taught at Stanford University[32]. Precision questioning enables Scrum Masters to solve complex problems, conduct in-depth analysis and make difficult decisions.

∆∆∆

SCRUM MASTERS ARE OPEN AND TRANSPARENT

Successful Scrum Masters are transparent in all forms of communication which plays an important role in quickly earning the trust of others and establishing a trustworthy relationship among team members. They say what they mean, and mean what they say; no hidden agendas, no games, no politics. This openness and transparency are not limited to the Scrum Masters' relationship to his/her Scrum Team, but also all external shareholders. The Scrum Master operates in such a way that it is easy for others to see what actions are performed[33]. Transparency further implies openness, communication, and accountability.

ΔΔΔ

SCRUM MASTERS ARE PROTECTIVE

Successful Scrum Masters are sensitive in detecting distractions and protective of the Scrum Team. As described in previous sections, one of the primary responsibilities of the Scrum Master is to block distractions so that the team is shielded against randomizations and therefore Scrum Team Members can focus on delivering business value in every sprint.

For example, in 2013, I was working as a Scrum Master of a Software Development Team who was responsible for a particular security component of a widely adopted web browser. The most important item in our *product backlog* was to create a thread model that will help the team determine potential attack patterns so that we would build appropriate protection mechanisms. This particular task was broken down into three sprints. In the middle of the second sprint, one of our partner teams asked me to update one of the UI components of the browser to improve its usability. According to my partner team, this was a high priority ask and should be executed immediately. I disagreed and openly explained to my counterpart why I would not distract my Scrum Team or deter them since they were about to deliver an important security feature for the privacy of my customers.

Furthermore, I did not even inform my Scrum Team about this ask to keep their focus on the current sprint. At the end of the third sprint, once the threat model was delivered as planned, I worked with my Product Owner to get the UI component prioritized for the upcoming sprints. As a result, I protected my Scrum Team from an unnecessary distraction which could have impeded the team's ability to deliver the committed increment of our final product.

$$\Delta\Delta\Delta$$

SCRUM MASTERS ARE COLLABORATIVE

Successful Scrum Masters have excellent collaboration skills, not only within their immediate Scrum Teams but also with other partners and stakeholders such as the Scrum Product Owner and Scrum Executive as well as customer representatives and partner teams. Collaboration requires leadership, although the form of leadership can be social within a decentralized and egalitarian group[34]. Teams that work collaboratively often access greater resources, recognition, and rewards when facing competition for finite resources[35]. Scrum Masters constantly seek opportunities to help Scrum Team Members achieve high levels of inter/intra-team collaboration.

$$\Delta\Delta\Delta$$

WHO SHOULD BE THE SCRUM MASTER?

Organizations that are new to Agile methodologies and Scrum Framework struggle initially to find a Scrum Master. However, Scrum Masters can be selected from many different existing roles/people in the team. Project Managers and Product Managers are natural candidates for being Scrum Masters. People coming from other backgrounds (such as Software Developers, Software Testers, Business Intelligence Engineers, Program Managers, Data Scientists, etc.) can successfully play the Scrum Master role if they choose to. As long as an individual has the characteristics, skills and competencies of a Scrum Master explained in this book, he/she can step up as the Scrum Master irrespective of what background he/she is coming from.

Some organizations promote their technical leaders to become the Scrum Masters. Even though this may sound like a good idea at the beginning, there are risks and inefficiencies associated with this approach. The Scrum Master is not necessarily a technical role and for that reason, picking a technical leader to be a Scrum Master limits the ability of the technical leader to achieve full potential in providing technical guidance to others. Teams who turn their technical leaders into Scrum Masters usually suffer from a technical delivery standpoint until someone else in the team steps up and compensates for the technical leadership gap.

Some other organizations promote their people managers to be the Scrum Masters. According to statistics, people managers make a great Scrum Master; however, it is important to make sure that the people managers do not directly manage the Scrum Team Members. Remember that Scrum Masters have no managerial authority over the Scrum Team Members, and mixing up Scrum Master authority with the managerial authority can lead to confusions and undesirable power dynamics within the Scrum Teams.

ΔΔΔ

IS SCRUM MASTER A FULL-TIME JOB?

Scrum Master is not a full-time job. In certain circumstances where the team members are not familiarized with the Agile methodologies, Scrum Master has to spend extra time coaching team members on Scrum Framework. As the team matures throughout multiple *sprint cycles*, the burden of the Scrum Master lessens; as a result, Scrum Team's load on the Scrum Master decreases, allowing the Scrum Master to focus on broader organizational goals and challenges. This not only enables the Scrum Master to have exposure to broader organization but also gives him/her the opportunity to influence multiple teams/products within the company.

Many successful Scrum Masters in the industry climb up the corporate ladder and become Scrum Product Owners or even Scrum Executives. The products they built, and the relationships they established along the way, enables Scrum Masters to excel in their careers, to enter circles of senior leadership, and be involved in the decision-making process.

CHAPTER 12: SCRUM PRODUCT OWNER

At the most basic level, the Scrum Product Owner is the *single threaded leader* who is responsible for maximizing the value of the products created by the Scrum Team[36]. To achieve this, the Scrum Product Owner has to play multiple roles including but not limited to business strategist, market analyst, customer liaison, product designer, project manager, and even finance manager.

Product Owners play two separate but related roles very successfully. First, Product Owners understand the needs of the customer as well as the stakeholders within the organization so that he/she can be their voice. The Product Owner is accountable and responsible for making sure that the right solution is developed for the customer. Second, the Product Owner clearly communicates to the Scrum Team what to build and in which order to build it. Furthermore, the Product Owner determines the quality bar which the product must meet to please its customers and satisfy the expectations of stake-holders.

In this chapter, you are going to learn, in detail, the unique role and responsibilities of successful Product Owners and how they operate.

△△△

RESPONSIBILITIES OF THE SCRUM PRODUCT OWNER

The Scrum Product Owner has six main responsibilities: collaborating with customer and stakeholders, collaborating with the Scrum Team, defining and enforcing acceptance criteria, creating and *grooming* the product backlog, managing economics of the product/project, and managing product planning activities.

Figure 8: Responsibilities of Product Owners

Let's look at each of these responsibilities in detail and understand what they mean as well as how you will apply them in your daily job.

ΔΔΔ

COLLABORATING WITH CUSTOMERS AND STAKEHOLDERS

The Product Owner is the single voice of all stakeholders including customers. Anybody who has an interest in the product is considered to be a *stakeholder*; such as the senior leadership team, program management, marketing, finance, sales, as well as Scrum Master and Scrum Team Members, users, partners, regulatory bodies, and most important of all, the customer. By collaborating closely with all stakeholders, the Product Owner creates a thorough vision that guides the Scrum Team through the product development lifecycle. Product Owners empathize with the customers' to come up with insights on the use cases as well as the needs of the customers, and they have the ability to turn those insights into requirements.

ΔΔΔ

COLLABORATING WITH THE SCRUM TEAM

Successful Product Owners establish and maintain a close relationship with the Scrum Team. Using Scrum Framework encourages building one feature at a time. This means that the team performs all necessary activities required to create a feature (such as design, code, test, etc.) on a continuous basis. That means that to be successful, Product Owners must engage with Scrum Teams on a constant basis. The engagement model that Product Owners must adopt is very different from the Product Ownership in the context of the traditional waterfall method.

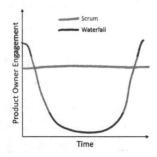

Figure 9: Continuous engagement

In Traditional Waterfall Model, customers and stakeholders are involved at the beginning of the project during the requirements phase, and then once again at the very end, during the delivery of the project. Development is done solely based on the gathered requirements and there is nothing for the stakeholders to review until the product is delivered.

On the contrary, Scrum Framework delivers self-contained value-add features in each sprint which involves customer and stakeholder engagement. For that reason, Product Owners must maintain a working relationship and a regular engagement with the Scrum Team so that each sprint gets the proper input from customers and stakeholders. Note that during these engagements, the Product Owner acts as a representative of the customers and the stakeholders. Many Product Owners fail to engage with Scrum Teams on a regular and continuous basis, which in turn prevents or delays the feedback flowing from the stakeholders to the Scrum Team, crippling the team's ability to react to the ever-changing nature of the customer requirements and stakeholder expectations.

ΔΔΔ

DEFINING AND ENFORCING ACCEPTANCE CRITERIA

The Product Owner is responsible and accountable for defining and enforcing the acceptance criteria for all *product backlog* items. The purpose of the acceptance criteria is to answer the following two fundamental questions: *did we build the right prod-*

uct and *did we build the product right.* Acceptance criteria represent the functional and non-functional requirements that, if met, all stakeholders will be satisfied with the product. It is important to note that the acceptance criteria (a.k.a. acceptance test) must be created before a *product backlog* item is picked up during the *sprint-planning* process by the Scrum Team. Without having some clear acceptance criteria in advance, Scrum Teams cannot know whether their deliverable is successful or not at the end of the sprint.

The Product Owner is also responsible and accountable for ensuring that the acceptance criteria are met. The test can be performed by the Product Owner himself/herself or by a dedicated test team or by another entity; however, the Product Owner is responsible for the final outcome and is the final judge whether the deliverable satisfies the expectations of the stakeholders.

$$\triangle\triangle\triangle$$

CREATING AND GROOMING PRODUCT BACKLOG

The Product Owner is the person responsible and accountable for managing the Product Backlog. Product Backlog management includes but is not limited to activities like:

- Creating Product Backlog items.
- Prioritizing the items in the Product Backlog to best achieve goals.
- Optimizing the value of the work the Scrum Team performs.
- Ensuring that the Product Backlog is visible, transparent, and clear to all stakeholder.
- Communicating to all stakeholders what Scrum Team will work on next.
- Ensuring the Scrum Team understands items in the Product Backlog in detail.

The Product Owner is also responsible for *grooming* the *product backlog* that includes activities such as creating the backlog item, coming up with a cost estimate for the items (with help from Scrum Team Members), and prioritizing the items so that Scrum Teams can focus on the most important items in their sprints.

$$\triangle\triangle\triangle$$

MANAGING THE ECONOMICS

Successful Product Owners have a profound understanding of various levels of economics including release-level economics, sprint-level economics, and product backlog economics. Product Owners consistently use economic trade-offs in their decision making.

Release-level economics can be explained using the following example. Assume that there is a newly identified feature that can increase revenue by 40% if the Scrum Team spends six weeks of extra effort leading to a 5% slip in the product schedule. Should the team trade a 5% slip in the product schedule for 40% extra revenue? The Product Owner makes such economic trade-offs to make sure that the right features are being built by the Scrum Team to maximize long-term objectives of the company.

The Product Owner is responsible for funding (or not funding) the next sprint of the Scrum Team. If the team is making good progress, Product Owner may choose to fund the next sprint. Otherwise, the Product Owner may choose not to fund the next sprint. Furthermore, once the Product Owner is satisfied with the state of the product, he/she may choose to stop funding any further development efforts and re-purpose the team to focus on other projects.

Sprint-level economics is about maximizing Return On Investment (ROI) for each sprint. Product Owners, Scrum Masters and every member of the Scrum Team should treat the company's money as they would their own money and be frugal about making economic decisions. This is especially important when determining whether or not to fund the next sprint. Will the value that the Scrum Team creates in the next sprint be worthy of spending the money to fund the sprint? The Product Owner is responsible for answering this question and deciding whether or not he/she will fund the next sprint.

Product-backlog economics is all about prioritizing the product backlog correctly so that the highest value items are executed first. As the economic value of each feature changes over time, the prioritization of those feature change too. And the Product Owner is responsible for making those re-prioritization decisions.

$$\triangle\triangle\triangle$$

MANAGING PRODUCT PLANNING ACTIVITIES

The Product Owner participates (sometimes drives) planning activities such as portfolio planning, product planning, release planning, and sprint planning. Portfolio planning is about working with stakeholders to best position the product in the portfolio backlog. Product planning is about envisioning the product. Release planning is about defining the content of the next release. Sprint planning is about defining the goal and deliverables of the upcoming sprint. The Product Owner is responsible and accountable for the successful completion of all planning activities.

△△△

COMPETENCIES OF THE PRODUCT OWNER

Successful Product Owners have certain common characteristics and competencies. First of all, Product Owners have very strong people skills. They are also knowledgeable of their domain. They have decision making authority which is balanced with a great sense of accountability for the end result. They are also inspirational, emotionally intelligent, open-minded, collaborative, bold and magnetic. In this chapter, we are going to examine in detail the competencies that every successful Product Owner should have.

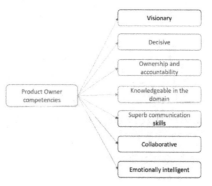

Figure 10: Competencies of Successful Product Owners

ΔΔΔ

PRODUCT OWNERS ARE DECISIVE

In the moment of decision, said Theodore Roosevelt, the best thing you can do is the right thing; the worst thing you can do is nothing. Product Owners are challenged with many decision points on a continuous basis; some are easy some are difficult. First of all, Product Owners must have decision making authority. Many organizations that are new to Scrum do not empower their Product Owners and require sign-off from senior leadership on the decisions that Product Owners make. This is a mistake. Product Owners should be empowered to the fullest extent, and this empowerment should be balanced with accountability rather than extra sign-off from senior leadership. Second, Product Owners must be decisive when it comes to making difficult decisions. They should be willing to make trade-offs between features, costs, date, and budget, and take justifiable risks when necessary.

ΔΔΔ

PRODUCT OWNERS ARE ACCOUNTABLE

Product Owners are the *owners* of the product. They have a strong sense of ownership which leads to accountability for the final results delivered by the Scrum Team. The Product Owner is responsible for making sure that the resources of the Scrum Team are utilized economically to create business value. The Product Owner uses his/her powers, such as prioritization of the product backlog, to influence what is being built by the Scrum Team and in what order. Furthermore, the Product Owner defines the acceptance criteria that the final product is evaluated against. Therefore, Product Owners are on the hook for ensuring that the final product is indeed successful.

ΔΔΔ

PRODUCT OWNERS ARE KNOWLEDGEABLE

Product Owners have a breadth knowledgebase; they have a *broad* understanding of the market and the domain in which the business is operating. They also have a unique product vision and how this product fits into the business model of the company as well as the positioning of this product in the market. Successful Product Owners do have passion, strength and enough knowledge to achieve their long-term vision. They are able to see beyond the ambiguity of today to build the tomorrow.

△△△

PRODUCT OWNERS HAVE SUPERB COMMUNICATION SKILLS

Product Owners are expected to communicate a clear direction in a way that all stakeholders can understand. Communication is a two-way street. Successful Product Owners ask *great questions* and help stakeholders to surface their underlying messages, intents, concerns, and driving forces in a way that is clearly understood by the Product Owner so that it can be communicated to the Scrum Team. Many Product Owners use a technique called *Socratic questioning.* Socratic questioning[37] is built on the disciplined practice of thoughtful questioning to enable the stakeholders to examine ideas and be able to determine the validity of those ideas. Socratic questioning is a form of disciplined questioning that can be used to pursue thought in many directions and for many purposes, including: to explore complex ideas, to get to the truth of things, to open up issues and problems, to uncover assumptions, to analyze concepts, to distinguish what we know from what we do not know, to follow out logical consequences of thought or to control discussions[38].

Furthermore, successful Product Owners also use another similar technique called *precision questioning* to get to the root of any particular group discussion. Precision questioning (PQ) is an intellectual toolkit for critical thinking[39] and problem-solving, grew out of a collaboration between Dennis Matthies and Dr. Monica Worline, while taught at Stanford University[40]. Precision questioning enables Scrum Masters to solve complex problems, conduct in-depth analysis and make difficult decisions.

Product Owners know how to connect emotionally with all stakeholders. They ask questions to exude genuine emotion and transparency. They carefully monitor how people feel. An emotional bond can only be formed when the Product Owner is actively present and honest at the moment. Product Owners are good storytellers. Research shows that as humans, we are wired to understand, connect and retain the information in stories much better. For example, my experiments show that character-driven stories with emotional content result in a better understanding of the key points a speaker wishes to make and enable better recall of these points weeks later. Regarding making an impact, this blows the standard PowerPoint presentation to bits. I advise business people to begin every presentation with a compelling, human-scale story[41].

ΔΔΔ

PRODUCT OWNERS ARE COLLABORATIVE

Successful Product Owners have excellent collaboration skills, not only within their immediate Scrum Teams but also other partners and stakeholders such as Scrum Master and Scrum Executive as well as customer representatives and partner teams. Collaboration requires leadership, although the form of leadership can be social within a decentralized and egalitarian group[42]. Teams that work collaboratively often access greater resources, recognition, and rewards when facing competition for finite resources[43].

ΔΔΔ

IS PRODUCT OWNER A FULL-TIME JOB?

Yes, Product Owner is indeed a full-time job. Product Owners have a variety of responsibilities throughout the development of each and every feature, interacting with internal and external stakeholders, Scrum Teams, Scrum Master, Scrum Executive, subject-matter-experts in the domain, as well as customer representatives and the customers.

They are on the hook for the successful development and launch of the product line. The responsibility is overwhelming and often considered to be too big for one person, depending on the size of the project. Trying to do it part-time would be setting yourself up for failure.

PRACTICAL CASE STUDIES: HOW TO USE YOUR TRAINING AND CERTIFICATE

Here are a few concrete examples that came from our students explaining how they took advantage of their training and utilized their certificate during a job interview as well as part of their daily jobs. We got permission from our students to share their stories. However, we do not disclose the names of our students or their companies to respect their privacy. Do you have a similar story to tell? We love to hear from you! Please reach out to us at contact@scrumassembly.org.

HOW AMY GOT A SENIOR PRODUCT MANAGER OFFER FROM HER DREAM COMPANY?

One of the students of International Scrum Assembly™ (let's call her Amy) is interviewing with a company for a Product Manager role in June 2018. Below is the reenacting of the dialogue she had with her interviewer. At certain parts of the dialogue, Emily (Program Director at International Scrum Assembly™) made remarks so that you can maximize your learnings/insights from Amy's experience.

INTERVIEWER

Let's say you are in charge of one of our product lines. Committed delivery date was six weeks ago, and according to the latest report, the team needs another four weeks to finish the job. How would you approach this situation?

AMY

Given that I'm in charge of the product line, I assume I'm the Product Owner. Is that correct?

INTERVIEWER

Yes.

AMY

First, I would like to listen to the previous Product Owner. Is he or she available for the transition?

INTERVIEWER

No. Assume that the previous Product Owner is not with the company anymore.

AMY

Okay. I would follow a threefold approach. First, I would reach out to the customer as well as other stakeholders (internal and external) and listen to their comments/concerns on the project. I expect they are having a bad experience with our company given that the product is already delayed. I would listen to their feedback and earn their trust. Second, I would reach out to my Scrum Masters and team members to listen to their story and understand their challenges/concerns, and earn their trust. Third, I would dig into the product backlog as well as sprint reviews to get myself familiarized with the product itself as well the journey that the team has been going through.

EMILY

Rather than rushing into finding a solution, Amy did a great job by stepping back and having a structured approach so that she can first assess the situation/problem correctly before attempting to solve it. Also, she emphasized earning the trust of customers, stakeholders and team members, which is the right thing to do. It takes a great deal of trust and partnership to turn around a failing project. Furthermore, she is referring to the company as "our company" which shows a strong sense of ownership and is a nice touch.

INTERVIEWER

That's a good start. Let's say the customer is extremely frustrated. Internal stakeholders are pissed and nervous because they got surprised by the six weeks delay and they have no confidence that the team can deliver it in the next four weeks. On the flip side, the team is a high-performance team and they are not aware of the frustration that the customer is going through.

AMY

One of the things I've learned is that transparency is key in recovering from a failing project. I assume that the customer is frustrated not only because the project is delayed, but also they were not communicated in advance about the upcoming delay. Is that a fair assumption?

INTERVIEWER

That's exactly right.

AMY

Alright. I would reach out to the customer and take responsibility (also apologize) for the delay as well as for the communication breakdown. In the meantime, I would work with my Scrum Masters to understand where we have failed. Have we not noticed that during the sprint review meetings? Have we not aware of customer expectations? When was the last time we delivered an iteration of our product? Etc. I would share my findings with the customer too for the sake of transparency.

INTERVIEWER

Do you think it is a good idea to air our dirty laundry?

AMY

I absolutely do. I would build trust with my customer by exposing the gaps I have identified in the process so that they understand why we failed in the first place as well as what we are doing differently going forward not to fail again.

EMILY

Amy made a very bold assertion here by saying "I absolutely do." She is right about the importance of transparency when it comes to building trust with customers while recovering from a failing project. However, the company may have its own reasons (e.g., contractual obligations, compliance requirements, possible legal actions, etc.) to not share those details with the customer. A wiser approach for Amy would be to still make a bold assertion while giving her interviewer a caveat.

INTERVIEWER

Okay. Now let's assume that the last time development teams delivered an iteration of the product was three months ago. Now what?

AMY

How long our sprints are?

INTERVIEWER

About eight weeks.

AMY

That is too long by any measure. I would organize

my sprints around one week, worst case, two weeks. That also points out the fact that we didn't do a good job breaking down the product into small iterations so that we deliver a shippable product every week or every other week. Had we organized our sprints correctly, we should have realized that the final delivery is at risk and we could take actions to mitigate that.

INTERVIEWER

So you think the main problem is long sprints?

AMY

That's definitely a problem. But I don't think that is the main problem. If the team (including the previous Product Owner, Scrum Master, Scrum Executive, and other stakeholders) think that it is acceptable to have eight weeks long sprints; that tells me that we have a more fundamental problem here that is lack of clear understanding of how teams should operate using an agile model. Our business cannot survive if we do not truly adopt the agile mentality.

INTERVIEWER

How do I know that you have the agile mentality?

AMY

I'm a certified Professional Scrum Product Owner. And I think I just pointed out one of the biggest gaps in the way your team operates.

(they both laugh)

(AMY continues)

You told me that the development team itself is a high-performance team. Everything that we talked about points to the fact that this is a misapplication of the Scrum Framework. I know how to fix this.

(at this point, the interviewer is smiling and jokingly makes the following comment)

EMILY
Even though I personally like the confidence that Amy had shown here especially when she said "I pointed out one of the biggest gaps in the way your team operates", some interviewers may find it a bit too aggressive, and some may even get into a defensive mode. Amy could have found other (more polished) ways of showing confidence to mitigate this risk.

INTERVIEWER
Who says this is a real problem? Maybe we are just talking hypothetically.

AMY
It sounded real. Besides, even if this were hypothetical, it is not too far from reality. I've seen projects fail exactly the same way you described for the same reasons that we root caused.

(they both smile and interviewer moves to the next question)

EMILY
This is a very successful interview. Amy has done a great job utilizing her Scrum training to get a Sr. Product Manager job offer from a Fortune 100 tech company. If you have any questions about this stu-

dent story, have any comments or suggestions, or you would like to share your own story; feel free to reach out to me at contact@scrumassembly.org.

CLOSING NOTES

Congratulations on completing your Scrum training. You are now ready to pass our official test and get yourself certified. Our accredited certificate will take your career to the next level. Before you take the final test, here are a few final notes.

- Do not worry about getting things perfect up-front. Scrum is all about continuous iteration and improvement.

- Do not expect Scrum adoption to be problem free. Your organization will encounter challenges that make using the Scrum framework difficult. Scrum makes visible dysfunctions and waste, therefore, enable organizations to realize their full potential.

- The status-quo is powerful and hard to break out of. Understand that it is human nature to resist to change. Help others by educating them on the fundamentals of Scrum and be patient. Don't fight with them, work with them.

- Scrum Teams, at regular intervals, reflects on how to become more effective, then tunes and adjusts its behavior accordingly. This is important for making continuous improvements.
- The most efficient and effective method of conveying information to and within a development team is a face-to-face conversation. Use face-to-face conversations when possible.

Congratulations once again. We are delighted to have you in our alumni network!

REFERENCES

[1] The Scrum Guide: The Definitive Guide to Scrum: https://www.scrumguides.org/docs/scrumguide/v1/scrum-guide-us.pdf

[2] Manifesto For Agile Software Development https://agilemanifesto.org/

[3] Ken Schwaber https://en.wikipedia.org/wiki/Ken_Schwaber

[4] Nolan Bushnell https://en.wikipedia.org/wiki/Nolan_Bushnell

[5] Agile https://en.wikipedia.org/wiki/Agile

[7] Essential Scrum: A Practical Guide to the Most Popular Agile Process. Kenneth Rubin - Addison-Wesley – 2013

[8] Principles Behind The Agile Manifesto. (n.d.). Retrieved from https://agilemanifesto.org/principles.html

[10] "Principles Behind The Agile Manifesto." Insert Name of Site in Italics. N.p., n.d. Web. https://agilemanifesto.org/principles.html.

[11] Tuckman's stages of group development https://en.wikipedia.org/wiki/Tuckman%27s_stages_of_group_development

[13] Jeff Bezos https://en.wikipedia.org/wiki/Jeff_Bezos

[14] The Science Behind Why Jeff Bezos's Two-pizza Team Rule Works, Janet Choi-Janet Choi- Google - http://blog.idonethis.com/two-pizza-team/

[15] The Two-pizza Rule and the Secret Of Amazon's Success. Alex Hern - https://www.theguardian.com/technology/2018/apr/24/the-two-pizza-rule-and-the-secret-of-amazons-success

[19] Invest (mnemonic) https://en.wikipedia.org/wiki/INVEST_(mnemonic)

[20] 13th Annual State Of Agile Survey | The Largest, Longest-running Agile Survey https://stateofagile.versionone.com/

[21] Alistair Cockburn https://en.wikipedia.org/wiki/Alistair_Cockburn

[25] Coach (sport) https://en.wikipedia.org/wiki/Coach_(sport)

[26] "Servant Leadership - Wikipedia." Insert Name of Site in Italics. N.p., n.d. Web. https://en.wikipedia.org/wiki/Servant_leadership.

[27] Sendjaya, Sen; Sarros, James C. (2002-09-01). "Servant Leadership: Its Origin, Development, and Application in Organizations". Journal of Leadership & Organizational Studies. 9 (2): 57–64. doi:10.1177/107179190200900205. ISSN 1548-0518.

[28] Bankwest Shut Senior Leaders in a Vault To Agree on Agile Ry Crozier https://www.itnews.com.au/news/bankwest-shut-senior-leaders-in-a-vault-to-agree-on-agile-515499

[29] "What is Socratic Questioning". Starting Point - Teaching Entry Level Geoscience. Carleton College. Retrieved March 31, 2018.

[30] Jacques Brunschwig, Geoffrey Ernest Richard Lloyd (eds), A Guide to Greek Thought: Major Figures and Trends, Harvard University Press, 2003, p. 233.

[31] Paul, Richard; Binker, A.J. (1990). Critical Thinking: What Every Person Needs To Survive in a Rapidly Changing World. Foundation for Critical Thinking. p. 360. ISBN 0-944583-08-3.

[32] 1995 – Precision Questioning (Published through the Stanford University Bookstore)

[33] Schnackenberg, Andrew K.; Tomlinson, Edward C. (March 2014). "Organizational transparency: a new perspective on managing trust in organization-

stakeholder relationships". Journal of Management. Sage. doi:10.1177/0149206314525202.

[34] Pence, Muneera U. "Graphic Design: Collaborative Processes = Understanding Self and Others." (lecture) Art 325: Collaborative Processes. Fairbanks Hall, Oregon State University, Corvallis, Oregon. 13 April 2006.

[35] Caroline S. Wagner and Loet Leydesdorff. Globalisation in the network of science in 2005: The diffusion of international collaboration and the formation of a core group Archived 2007-08-25 at the Wayback Machine.

[36] "7 Key Product Owner Responsibilities | Lucidchart Blog." Insert Name of Site in Italics. N.p., n.d. Web. https://www.lucid-chart.com/blog/product-owner-roles-and-responsibilities.

[37] "What is Socratic Questioning". Starting Point - Teaching Entry Level Geoscience. Carleton College. Retrieved March 31, 2018.

[38] Jacques Brunschwig, Geoffrey Ernest Richard Lloyd (eds), A Guide to Greek Thought: Major Figures and Trends, Harvard University Press, 2003, p. 233.

[39] Paul, Richard; Binker, A.J. (1990). Critical Thinking: What Every Person Needs To Survive in a Rapidly Changing World. Foundation for Critical Thinking. p. 360. ISBN 0-944583-08-3.

[40] 1995 – Precision Questioning (Published through the Stanford University Bookstore)

[41] Why Your Brain Loves Good Storytelling - Ideas And Advice (n.d.). Retrieved from https://hbr.org/2014/10/why-your-brain-loves-good-storytelling

[42] Pence, Muneera U. "Graphic Design: Collaborative Processes = Understanding Self and Others." (lecture) Art 325: Collaborative Processes. Fairbanks Hall, Oregon State University, Corvallis, Oregon. 13 April 2006.

[43] Caroline S. Wagner and Loet Leydesdorff. Globalisation in the network of science in 2005: The diffusion of international collaboration and the formation of a core group Archived 2007-08-25 at the Wayback Machine.